Trauma Shift

Have You Got What It Takes to Be an ER Nurse?

by Lisa Thompson

Compass Point Books ✦ Minneapolis, Minnesota

First American edition published in 2009 by
Compass Point Books
151 Good Counsel Drive
P.O. Box 669
Mankato, MN 56002-0669

Editor: Anthony Wacholtz
Designer: Ashlee Suker
Art Director: LuAnn Ascheman-Adams
Creative Director: Joe Ewest
Editorial Director: Nick Healy
Managing Editor: Catherine Neitge
Content Adviser: Pamela D. Wolters, RN-BSN,
             Staff Nurse Emergency Department
             Immanuel-St. Joseph's Mayo Health System
             Mankato, Minnesota

Editor's note: To best explain careers to readers, the author has
created composite characters based on extensive interviews and research.

This book was manufactured with paper containing
at least 10 percent post-consumer waste.

Library of Congress Cataloging-in-Publication Data
Thompson, Lisa.
  Trauma shift : have you got what it takes to be an ER nurse? / by Lisa Thompson.
     p. cm.
  Includes index.
  ISBN 978-0-7565-4078-4 (library binding)
1. Emergency nursing—Juvenile literature. 2. Hospitals—Emergency services—
Juvenile literature. I. Title.
  RT120.E4V35 2009
  616.02'5—dc22   2008038461

Image Credits: Scott Leman/Shutterstock, 14 (bottom); Leah-Anne Thompson/
Shutterstock, 16 (bottom); Robert Simon/iStockphoto, 20 (bottom); Coenders/
iStockphoto, 25 (top); Alexey Ivanov/iStockphoto, 33 (bottom left); jkbowers/
iStockphoto, 37 (bottom). All other images are from one of the following royalty-
free sources: Big Stock Photo, Dreamstime, Istock, Photo Objects, Photos.com,
and Shutterstock. Every effort has been made to contact copyright holders of any
material reproduced in this book. Any omission will be rectified in subsequent
printings if notice is given to the publishers.

Visit Compass Point Books on the Internet at *www.compasspointbooks.com*
or e-mail your request to *custserv@compasspointbooks.com*

Table of Contents

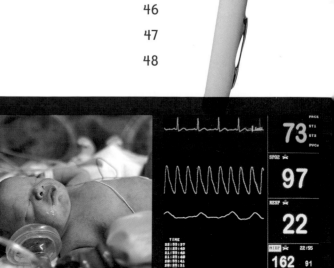

Trauma Alert

I'm organizing the transfer of an elderly patient with a broken arm to X-ray when a call comes in on my pager.

Along with an emergency room (ER) doctor, I rush to the helipad. The helicopter doors open, and the patient, a 19-year-old male lying on a stretcher, is rushed into the hospital. From the amount of blood and his obvious injuries, I can tell that he is in serious condition.

MAJOR TRAUMA—
HELIPAD—ARRIVAL
2 MINUTES.

*The word **trauma** describes a wound that occurs during a sudden physical accident and can produce shock.*

On the way down to the ER, the paramedic begins his report: "High-speed car accident … unconscious at the scene … extensive blood loss." My eyes scan the patient, looking for visible injuries.

He appears to have broken bones in both arms and in one of his legs. There is a deep laceration on his face, and he has glass all over his hair. His head (supported by a neck brace) looks swollen.

Once inside the ER, we transfer the patient to a resuscitation bay (resus bay). We are joined by the rest of the trauma team and an anesthesiologist. We try to stabilize the patient as our team's assessment begins.

The team listens carefully as Dr. Joan Ellis gives a complete verbal assessment of the patient. After I cut off the patient's clothing, two radiographers bring in the X-ray machine so we can check his bones and lungs.

An X-ray shows where the bone is broken.

5

The senior team nurse fills out a trauma response sheet as the team leader directs the team members. Another nurse checks and records the patient's vital signs: "Blood pressure 81/54 ... heart rate 130 ... respiratory rate 26 ... oxygen stats 92 percent."

Trauma response sheet

I scan the patient's body to see where I can access a vein with an intravenous (IV) cannula. Placing a cannula in the vein allows me to give the patient warm fluids, medications, and blood products.

We check the patient's heart rate, blood pressure, and other vital signs.

My first attempt to place a needle in a vein fails because his blood pressure is low from hemorrhaging. The tension is high when a patient is injured this badly because every second counts. I remain calm and try to place two IV lines in his forearm. I'm unable to find a suitable vein there but manage to find a site in his wrist instead.

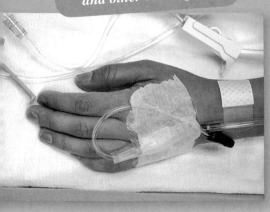

The doctor continues the assessment. She notes that the patient is losing a lot of blood and we still don't know all his injuries. His blood pressure is low, and his heart rate and breathing are fast.

He needs to be stabilized as quickly as possible. I grab a bag of blood from the coolers in the resus bay. I then hook it up to a rapid infuser—a machine that heats up the blood as it pushes it into the patient's veins.

The EKG machine prints the heart rate.

B (Rh -)

O (Rh+)
O (Rh -)

Doctors and nurses have to make sure they use the correct blood type.

Vital Signs

There are six standard vital signs to check a person's basic health in most medical situations:

blood pressure—How well is the blood moving around the body?

heart rate—How many heart beats per minute?

respiratory rate—How many breaths per minute?

oxygen saturation level—How much oxygen is in the blood?

temperature—Is it within normal range?

GCS (Glasgow Coma Scale)—How alert is the person?

The Team in Action

Everyone is busy working as a team to assess the patient and to gather information that could change second by second.

My mind is full of questions: Are the IVs running and working? There is bruising around his abdomen. Is he bleeding internally? How deep are the cuts on his legs and arms?

1. The patient cannot breathe properly, so we prepare to put a breathing tube down his throat and into his lungs to allow a ventilator to breathe for him.

2. The doctor calls out the medications and the doses she wants given to the patient. I prepare the syringe to administer them. The ventilator is ready.

Getting the right dose of medication is crucial.

PUN FUN Nurses are patient people.

8

The doctor signals that it is time to administer the medications to sedate and paralyze the patient. This is so the patient feels no pain. The doctor puts the tube down the patient's throat, and his chest starts to rise and fall more easily with the help of the ventilator. A chest X-ray is taken to make sure the tube is in the right place and inflating both lungs correctly.

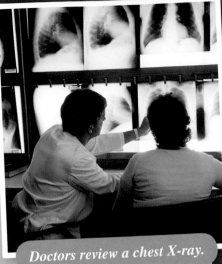

Doctors review a chest X-ray.

The patient is now stable enough to transfer to radiology for further scans to check for possible neck and head injuries.

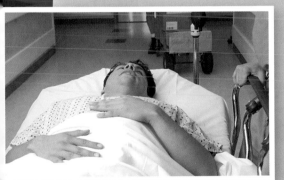

As the patient is moved to another department, I am ready for the next emergency. This time, it is a teenager suffering from a dislocated shoulder. I begin by checking her vital signs. It's all systems go again.

OK, who's next on the list?

Why I Became an Emergency Nurse

It wasn't until after I finished high school that I thought about nursing as a career. The only time I had ever been to a hospital was after I broke my arm during a soccer game when I was 9 years old. After I graduated from high school, I went traveling and met someone who was working as a nurse for an international aid group called Médecins Sans Frontières (Doctors Without Borders). He was part of a disaster response team.

It was the first time I had ever heard of an emergency nurse. When I returned from traveling, I decided to enroll at a university to get a bachelor's degree in nursing.

Before they become emergency nurses, students learn by spending time in the practice rooms.

Pediatricians specialize in taking care of babies and children.

While studying, I was able to work in many hospital departments— general wards, pediatrics, intensive care, surgery, oncology (an area that treats people who have cancer), and the ER. As soon as I hit the ER, I knew it was for me.

I like the ER because of the fast pace and variety of cases. No two days—or even two hours—are ever the same! One minute you can be stitching up a cut, and the next you are reviving a patient who has just had a heart attack. It's not always that extreme, but it can be. You never know what is going to come through the door.

There is also a lot of teamwork needed in the ER. When a serious case arrives, there is a lot of pressure to assess and stabilize the patient as quickly as possible. It really gets your heart racing. You have to react quickly, yet calmly, in what might be a life-or-death situation.

11

The main reason I got into nursing was that I would be able to use my skills all over the world to help others. For me, that's what makes nursing exciting and fulfilling. Next year, I am going to Africa on my first Doctors Without Borders assignment. I can't wait!

Emergency nursing also appeals to me because I like working directly with people. You get to meet all kinds of people in the ER. Along with treating patients, you need to be able to work with other emergency nurses as well.

What is emergency nursing?

Emergency nursing is a specialty in which nurses care for patients in an emergency or in a critical phase of

Excellent communication skills are a must.

Emergency nurses are team players.

injury or illness. Emergency nurses deal with a wide range of patients, from life-threatening emergencies and traumas to minor emergency illnesses and mental health issues. They work in a high-pressure environment where skill, quick action, and teamwork are essential for successful care.

Emergency nurses are at the front line of the hospital's contact with the community. They often deal with patients who have injuries or illnesses that are not yet diagnosed. They need a broad range of nursing skills, as well as the ability to react and treat patients quickly and confidently.

✔ CHECK LiST

Qualities you need to be a good emergency nurse:

- ☐ the ability to stay calm in a crisis
- ☐ the ability to think and react quickly
- ☐ broad clinical knowledge
- ☐ flexible approach to work
- ☐ strong teamwork skills
- ☐ excellent communication skills
- ☐ willingness to constantly learn
- ☐ lots of energy/good physical fitness
- ☐ strong stomach for the sight of blood and injuries

The Emergency Room

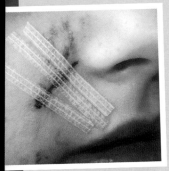

The role of a hospital emergency room is to care for medical emergencies. The ER staff addresses any illnesses or injuries requiring urgent attention.

One of the most challenging and amazing aspects of working in the ER is the vast range of conditions that arrive on a daily basis. No other medical specialty sees the variety of conditions that are present at an ER.

Top five reasons for coming to the ER

1. chest pains—heart attacks, indigestion, panic attacks

2. falls

3. closed head injuries (skull is intact but there is damage done on the inside)

4. abdominal pains—kidney stones, appendicitis

5. motor vehicle accident injuries

Other common conditions that bring people to the ER:

- sports injuries
- broken bones and cuts from accidents and falls
- burns
- uncontrolled bleeding
- breathing difficulties (asthma, pneumonia, etc.)
- strokes or loss of function in the arms or legs

- loss of vision or hearing
- unconsciousness
- confusion/fainting
- drug overdoses
- persistent vomiting
- food poisoning
- allergic reactions from insect bites, food, or medications
- complications from diseases
- high fevers

Rush hours

Weekends and nights are the busiest times in hospital emergency rooms. That's when people are not in their usual routine and are more likely to hurt themselves playing sports or attempting "do-it-yourself" jobs. Also, once the sun goes down, the darkness makes things more dangerous.

MIST

When paramedics bring a patient to the ER, they call ahead and provide essential information so the trauma team is ready.

M = Mechanism—how the injury happened

I = Injury—what the injury is

S = Signs and symptoms— what's happening to the patient's body, both internally and externally

T = Treatment—how the patient was cared for at the site of the injury

ER areas

Most emergency rooms have separate areas for the conditions that need to be treated. These include:

- trauma (resuscitation) area—for patients suffering life-threatening conditions
- pediatric area—specially designed and equipped for children
- psychiatric area—for patients with mental health problems
- subacute (minor) injuries unit—for patients with easily treatable injuries or illnesses
- consultation area—to discuss treatment with patients and relatives

Who's Who in the Emergency Room

There are a lot of medical personnel involved in running an ER. Here are just some of the nurses you might meet there.

Emergency nurse

Emergency nurses have expert knowledge and specific training. They work as a team with doctors and treat the variety of patients at the ER.

ER doctors and nurses work side by side.

Triage nurse

For any patient, the first person they see is the triage nurse. He or she checks vital signs and ask questions to assess how urgent the person's condition is. This critical assessment must be done in 90 seconds or less, so only highly skilled and experienced nurses do this job. He or she also directs patients to the appropriate area of the ER.

Registered nurse (RN)

A registered nurse has earned a diploma in nursing and has passsed an exam to become a licensed nurse. RNs may make suggestions regarding medical care and may fill many of the nursing positions in any ER.

Nurse practitioner

This senior nurse works alongside the triage nurse. Nurse practitioners begin treatment while people are waiting. They can order X-rays, prescribe and administer pain relief and drugs, take blood, begin IV fluids, plaster and suture—all without a doctor.

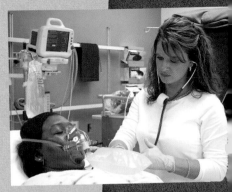

In-charge/coordinator nurse

The in-charge/coordinator nurse oversees the entire ER to keep patients flowing through and to avoid any bottlenecks.

The coordinator nurse keeps an eye on the big picture in the ER.

What about ER doctors?

ER doctors are ultimately responsible for patients. They make the decisions regarding a patient's diagnosis, treatment, and care. Only they can order specialized tests, like a CT scan.

17

How an Emergency Room Works

1

Clerical staff will register your personal details and obtain any old medical records.

2

When it's your turn, a nurse will take you into an examination room where he or she will ask more questions and assess your symptoms. The nurse may take urine and blood samples or perform an EKG. He or she will also check your vital signs.

3

Once the nurse has finished, a doctor will visit to get a more detailed medical history and assess the situation. Doctors use a system called differential diagnosis. This involves making a list of possible causes for your symptoms and choosing the most likely one based on evidence from physically examining you. They confirm this diagnosis with tests and begin treatment. There will be a further medical review to make sure the treatment is working. If it isn't, then the diagnosis may have been incorrect, and the doctor will reassess the situation.

4

If you need to stay in the hospital, you will be moved to the appropriate ward, or department of the hospital. Otherwise, you will be treated and discharged from the ER. You may receive a referral to another hospital or organization if any follow-up care is required.

TRAUMA & EMERGENCY UNIT

When you arrive at the ER, the triage nurse will rapidly assess how urgent your condition is.

Triage levels

Emergency room patients receive treatment in order of the seriousness of their emergency, not their time of arrival. The triage nurse categorizes patients according to the Emergency Severity Index:

Level 1	emergent	patients with unstable vital signs who require immediate attention (cardiac arrest, critical injuries, uncontrolled bleeding)
Level 2	urgent	patients with stable vital signs but exhibit life-threatening symptoms (signs of heart attacks or strokes, high fevers in very young babies)
Level 3	acute	patients who develop sudden illnesses or injuries within one or two days (mild abdominal pain, dehydration)
Level 4	routine	patients with conditions that are not life-threatening (minor lacerations, minor injuries that may require lab work or an X-ray)
Level 5		patients who are stable and require no immediate treatment

Tools of the Trade

Emergency rooms are full of equipment that emergency nurses need to know how to use.

Stethoscope

A stethoscope lets a nurse or doctor listen for heart and breathing sounds inside a person's chest. Abnormal heart rhythms can indicate possible problems or even heart failure. Stethoscopes are also used to listen to bowel sounds in the abdomen. Used with a blood pressure cuff (sphygmomanometer), a stethoscope is also used to take blood pressure readings.

Electrocardiogram machine (EKG or ECG)

This machine shows the electrical activity in the heart. It has 10 wires connected to 10 pads, which are stuck to the patient's chest. It gives trauma teams detailed information about which parts of the heart are working. It takes about three minutes for the test to be completed.

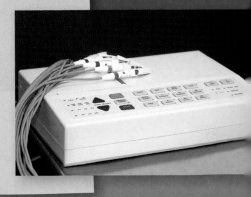

Cardiac monitor

A cardiac monitor gives a visual display of the rhythm of the heart. The monitor checks to see if the heart is beating. It also checks to see how fast the heart is beating. An alarm rings if the heart rate goes above or below a specific range. The monitor also measures blood pressure and the amount of oxygen in the blood. It is for monitoring patients who have already been stabilized.

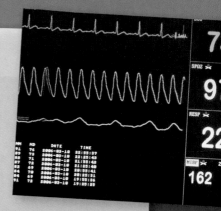

Orthopedic equipment

Orthopedic equipment is for repairing breaks and sprains. It includes plaster and fiberglass materials to splint breaks. There may also be pre-made splints for specific joints, shoulder slings, and cast cutters for removing casts.

Suture tray

This tray contains sterile equipment needed for stitching lacerations. It includes needle holders, forceps, sterile towels, scissors, and small bowls to hold antiseptic solutions.

Resuscitation bay

A resuscitation (resus) bay contains the equipment needed when a heart stops beating (a cardiac arrest). This situation requires immediate lifesaving steps. Items found in the resus bay include:

defibrillator: electrical device that shocks the heart back into beating or to a normal rhythm

endotracheal intubation equipment: used to place a tube down a person's throat to help him or her breath or to allow respiration equipment to take over the job of breathing for the patient

central vein cannulas: small tubes placed in central veins so that medications and fluids can reach the heart and important organs more quickly

cardiac drugs: strong drugs required to restart the heart or return it to a more stable rhythm

chest tube tray: holds the equipment needed to put in a chest tube to expand a collapsed lung

Computerized (Axial) Tomography (CT or CAT) scan

CT scans are more detailed than X-rays and show the differences between solids and soft tissue in the body. A CT scan on the abdomen shows the ribs, spine, and any gases. Internal organs such as kidneys and liver can also be seen.

X-rays and scans

Emergency nurses often refer patients to the radiology department for X-rays or scans to better determine the extent of an injury or illness. X-rays are the most basic scans to see, for example, if a bone is broken or a tissue is damaged.

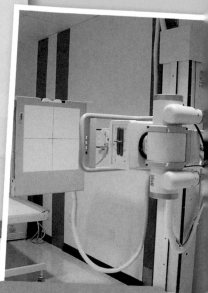

A radiographer is a person who specializes in X-rays and scans.

MRI (Magnetic Resonance Imaging)

An MRI is the most advanced and detailed scan, which can show the difference between tissue types (for example, the gray and white matter in the brain). It is used for diagnosing tumors, soft tissue injuries, spine and brain injuries, and other serious injuries.

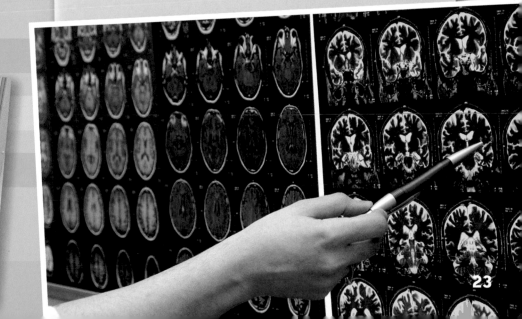

23

Special rooms

The eye room is a specialized room used just for treating eyes. It contains slit lamps (to check eye function), eye tests, refrigerators with various eye drops, dressings, and eye medicines.

The ear, nose, and throat room has equipment for treating nosebleeds and to remove objects from the ear, nose, and throat. It has a reclining chair and equipment like mouth guards and otoscopes, which are used to look in the ears.

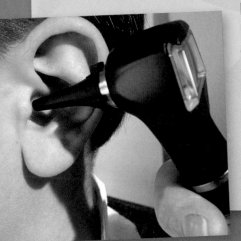

Diagnostic testing

Emergency nurses collect other samples and refer patients for further diagnostic testing, such as blood and urine analysis, ultrasounds, X-rays, CT scans, and MRIs.

PUN FUN

The nurse was nervous about giving a vaccination, but she gave it her best shot.

Blood testing

When blood tests are required, a nurse draws samples of a patient's blood and puts them into color-coded tubes, each for a different test. The ER team receives the results in a matter of minutes.

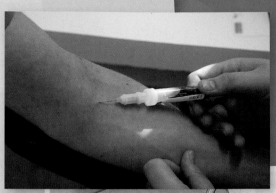

There are three standard blood tests:

1. *Full Blood Count (FBC)*
The FBC measures
   - red blood cells to check for anemia

   - number and type of white blood cells to see if an infection is present

Red blood cells

   - number of platelets (parts of the blood necessary to stop bleeding)

2. *Electrolytes, Urea, and Creatinine (EUC)*
The serum (liquid) in blood is tested. It shows how well major organs, like the kidneys and liver, are working

3 *Coagulopathy (COAGs)*
The blood's clotting ability is tested

Out in the Field

Emergency and disaster nurses work all over the world. They provide relief where there is war, disaster, poverty, or hardship—wherever emergency medical care is needed.

International Federation of Red Cross and Red Crescent Societies

The International Federation of Red Cross and Red Crescent Societies is the world's largest relief organization. The organization, made up of two societies, provide relief to countries all over the world. They help countries suffering from natural disasters, poverty, or health emergencies.

Nurses play an important role in the success of the Red Cross and Red Crescent organizations. In the American Red Cross alone, more than 30,000 nurses are involved with many of the services that the organizations provide, such as disaster relief and blood collection.

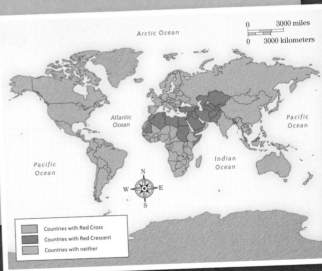

Arctic Ocean

Atlantic Ocean

Pacific Ocean

Pacific Ocean

Indian Ocean

0   3000 miles
0   3000 kilometers

Countries with Red Cross
Countries with Red Crescent
Countries with neither

Médecins Sans Frontières (MSF)/ Doctors Without Borders

The MSF is an international, medical-humanitarian organization. It delivers emergency aid to people affected by war, epidemics, or natural disasters. It also helps those without health care in more than 70 countries around the world.

In emergency and disaster situations, the MSF:

- provides essential health care
- performs surgeries
- carries out vaccinations
- operates feeding centers
- constructs wells
- provides clean drinking water
- provides shelter materials (blankets, plastic sheets)

The Royal Flying Doctors Service (RFDS)

RFDS provides free emergency and medical care to people who live, work, or travel in regional and remote Australia. It is the oldest and largest airborne health service of its kind in the world.

All of the RFDS's 50 specially modified King Air and PC-12 aircraft are like flying emergency rooms. They carry medical equipment such as:

- resuscitation devices
- neonatal incubators (for newborn babies)
- batteries to provide power
- medical oxygen
- suction system
- special communication systems

A team of one pilot and one nurse carries out the majority of flights. A doctor will assist on flights involving seriously ill patients. The RFDS also provides medical advice to people.

History of Nursing

The world's first nursing school was in India in 250 B.C. The school only trained men. Nursing was mainly done by men during the Middle Ages (500–1500 A.D.).

Other male organizations during the Middle Ages, like the Alexian Brothers and Knights Hospitalers, provided nursing and medical care for the poor and sick.

Even up until 1900, male nurses and nursing schools for men were quite common. It was only after 1900 that organizations began training female nurses.

Nursing in the 1900s

In the early 1900s, hospitals provided nursing education—not colleges and universities. Student nurses would work 10 to 12 hours a day—seven days a week—and they only devoted a few hours each day to studies.

New nursing students often worked as maids by washing dishes and cleaning at the hospital. When the supervisor determined the student was ready, he or she would be assigned to more duties involving patients.

After graduating, the nurses tried to find work in their field. The most common job was to work in the home of a patient. On top of caring for the patient, the nurse would often perform housekeeping duties as well. Some of these tasks included sweeping, mopping, cooking meals, washing clothes, and even cleaning chimneys.

World War II

Nurses took on a different role during World War II. Instead of caring for patients in a hospital or in someone's home, nurses risked their lives by traveling to the battlefields to tend to wounded soldiers. More than 200 U.S. nurses died during their service in the war.

After the war, the demand for nurses increased. Education was more widely available for students interested in nursing programs. Students also started specializing in various areas of nursing. In the following decades, nurses were given more responsibility with their patients. Over time, with the development of better equipment and technology, nursing has evolved into a reliable health care field.

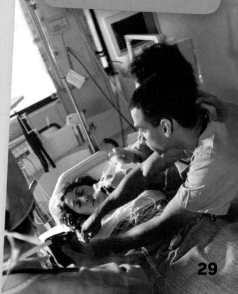

Saving lives: a job for men and women

Florence Nightingale promoted nurse education.

Florence Nightingale (1820–1910)

Florence Nightingale was a pioneer in modern nursing. Her most famous contribution to nursing was during the Crimean War in 1854. She and 38 volunteer nurses that she had trained went to Turkey to look after British soldiers. The conditions at the army hospital were dreadful. Nightingale and her nurses cleaned the hospital and reorganized patient care. This started Nightingale's quest to educate people on the importance of sanitary conditions in hospitals.

In 1860, Nightingale set up the Nightingale Training School for nurses. She spent her life promoting and organizing the development of nursing. She set a great example for nurses everywhere with her compassion, commitment to patient care, and efficient hospital administration.

Clara Barton
(1821–1912)

During the American Civil War, Clara Barton set up an agency to distribute supplies to wounded soldiers. At first she rode in Army ambulances to nurse soldiers back to health. Then, in July 1862, she began traveling to the front lines, risking her own safety to care for the wounded at some of the grimmest battlefields of the war.

After the war, Barton went to Europe and became involved with the International Red Cross. When she returned to the United States, she successfully campaigned for the Red Cross to be supported by the government. She became the first president of the U.S. branch of the Red Cross Society.

The first RN

Ellen Dougherty (1844–1919) was the first registered nurse in the world. She trained at Wellington Hospital in New Zealand—the first country in the world to regulate nursing nationally. From that time, laws defined the scope of practice and a standard of care for nursing. Nurses became legally responsible and accountable for their practice.

PUN FUN The nurse went to art school to learn to draw blood.

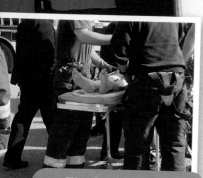

Firefighters assist paramedics in transporting a patient.

Patient Update

The X-rays and scans revealed that the patient had two broken bones in both arms, a broken femur (thigh bone) in his right leg, multiple fractures around his eyes, and a punctured liver causing a large loss of blood. He is now in a serious but stable condition in the intensive care unit (ICU), after having had surgery to repair his liver.

Next I attend to a young girl with a dislocated shoulder. I administer pain relief medication and arrange an X-ray to check which way the shoulder is dislocated. After sedation, the girl's shoulder is put back into the right position. She is discharged four hours after waking up because she has no other symptoms.

ICU—monitoring patients as they rest and recover.

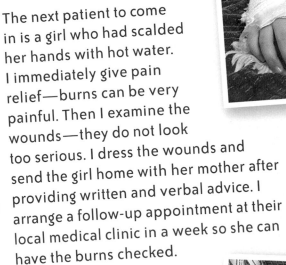

The next patient to come in is a girl who had scalded her hands with hot water. I immediately give pain relief—burns can be very painful. Then I examine the wounds—they do not look too serious. I dress the wounds and send the girl home with her mother after providing written and verbal advice. I arrange a follow-up appointment at their local medical clinic in a week so she can have the burns checked.

I finish the documentation for the girl with the burns and file her notes. In the ER, each case is written up at the time—not at the end of the shift. That way, notes are more accurate and complete.

Finally I'm off to lunch. What a morning!

The World of Nursing

Nurses practice in a wide range of settings:

- pharmaceutical companies doing research
- hospitals
- schools
- clinics
- correctional centers or prisons
- cruise ships
- sporting events
- film locations and movie sets
- camps
- nursing homes
- health care and insurance industries (as advisers)

Community nurse

There are more than 70 areas of nursing that require special training. Some of these are:

- burns
- community health
- infectious diseases
- midwifery
- nurse consultancy (educating other nurses or assessing policy)
- psychiatric care
- rehabilitation
- surgery

Midwifery

Levels of nursing

- Licensed practical nurses (LPNs): Have between one and two years of training and work under the direction of physicians and registered nurses; also known as licensed vocational nurses (LVNs)

- Registered nurses (RNs): Have earned a bachelor's degree, an associate degree, or a diploma from a nursing program

- Advanced practice nurses (APNs): Have earned a master's degree in nursing and/or have completed additional advanced training; work with doctors to evaluate and treat patients; can prescribe medications and order laboratory tests

- Doctorates of nursing practice (DNPs): Have earned a doctorate degree (not the same as a medical doctorate); continue providing care to patients

What's your focus?

There are more than 2.5 million nurses throughout the United States. Nearly 60 percent of these nurses work in hospitals.

There are many general areas in which a nurse can specialize, such as emergency, mental health, and rehabilitation. Other nurses focus on particular diseases conditions, such as addictions, developmental disabilities, and genetics. Others concentrate in areas dealing with specific organs or body parts, such as orthopedics, gynecology, and dermatology.

True Stories From the ER

In the years I've worked as a nurse in the ER, I've seen some rather unusual cases.

Man versus cactus

A 40-year-old man was at a garden party when an overly adventurous dance move landed him head-first into a cactus patch. He came in with rather sore hands and arms that were covered in spines. Once we gave him some painkillers, he was much happier and even sat still as we pulled out the spines.

Macaroni up the nose

A 12-year-old girl, accompanied by her embarrassed mother, came into the ER with a piece of macaroni stuck up her nose. When I asked her why she'd put it there, she told me she wanted to see if she could breathe through it. Well, turns out she could. But then she realized that she couldn't get it back out. Using a pair of tweezers, a nurse was able to remove the macaroni.

Bug crazy

Every now and then, someone comes into the ER with a bug of some kind in his or her ear. If the bug is still alive, we treat the patient pretty quickly because he or she is probably annoyed from all the buzzing! The quickest way to get the bug out is to pour olive oil in first (unfortunately we do have to kill the bug so it doesn't crawl in farther). Then we remove it with a forceps.

What's the emergency?

Sometimes people come to the emergency room with a situation that is not considered serious. Other times, the person does not need to come to the hospital at all. One such case was a teen who came to the emergency room at 2 A.M. What was his condition? He complained of belly button lint!

PUN FUN

The orange went to the emergency room because it wasn't peeling very well.

Back in the ER That Afternoon

1 P.M.
The flow of patients continues throughout the afternoon and into the early evening. A young girl arrives by ambulance after falling in a park. She requires stitches in her hand. I clean the area and give her an anesthetic before I grab the suture tray and begin stitching.

3 P.M.
A man who fell off his ladder now has a swollen ankle. I ask him questions about his medical history and how the accident happened. Like all other patients who are conscious, I run through a series of questions and check if he is currently taking any medication.

PUN FUN
One tonsil said to the other, "Get dressed—the doctor's taking us out tonight!"

I administer some pain relief. A doctor assesses the patient, checking the X-rays that were ordered. It doesn't look too bad—otherwise an orthopedic surgeon would be called to review the X-rays.

4 P.M.
The X-rays reveal the man has broken two bones in his ankle. The bones don't need to be set, so I plaster his ankle and arrange additional pain medication for him to take home.

DIARY

NOTES

PROJECTS

INFORMATION

FINANCIAL

ADDRESSES

5 P.M.
My pager goes off—MAJOR
TRAUMA AMBULANCE BAY.
A woman has badly hurt her
leg after falling down a cliff.
She has lost a lot of blood and is
unconscious. She has bruising and
swelling on the left side of her
head and cuts over her face
and body.

We rush her to the resus bay
where the team works for
over an hour to stabilize her
condition. She is intubated;
the ABCDE survey is
carried out; the bleeding is
controlled; and brain, spine,
abdomen, and pelvic scans
are done.

Primary survey

A primary survey is the first thing done for every ER patient,
without exception. It is an internationally recognized system of
the most important checks to keep someone alive. Only when A
has been checked and dealt with will the ER nurse move on to B,
and so on.

A = Airway—is it clear?
B = Breathing—can the person breathe?
C = Circulation—check heart rate, blood pressure, blood loss, etc.
D = Disability—what is the patient's level of consciousness?
E = Exposure—check temperature (remove clothes if necessary
      for treatment).

Ambulance bay

7 P.M.
My eight-hour shift has ended.
I have had two major traumas and
seen 17 patients in all. I brief the next
shift's emergency nurse as I hand over
patients who are still under ER care.

Now I am off to play a game of
basketball, where I also double as the
first-aid officer. Tomorrow I will be
back in the ER, ready for the next
emergency. For me, every work day
is unpredictable and exciting!

Abdominal CT scan

Every Minute Counts

In a medical emergency, having someone immediately available with basic first-aid training can often be the difference between life and death. When oxygen is cut off from the brain (from drowning or choking, for example), irreversible brain damage begins to occur within three to four minutes.

Every minute counts!

Basic first aid

First aid is the initial care of the ill or injured. The aim of first aid is to:

1. preserve life

2. prevent the injury or illness from becoming worse

3. reassure the ill or injured before medical help arrives (if needed)

Heart matters

Approximately 75 percent of cardiac arrests occur in people's homes, but only 22 percent of patients receive CPR (cardiopulmonary resuscitation) before emergency services arrive.

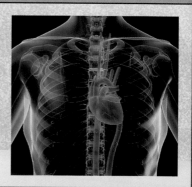

A basic first aid kit should include:

- Absorbant and cold compresses
- Antiseptic wipes
- Painkillers
- Nonlatex gloves

- Scissors
- Sterile gauze
- Bandages
- Cloth tape

Additional items can include tweezers, hand sanitizer, a blanket, a thermometer, an ice pack, first-aid cream, and antibiotics.

Things to remember when making an emergency call

Remain calm when speaking to the operator so you can answer questions correctly and clearly.

Speak slowly and loudly to the operator.

"Where is your emergency?" and "What is your emergency?" are the most important pieces of information you can give an emergency operator in a call.

EMERGENCY

Follow These Steps to Become an ER Nurse

Step **1**

Finish high school with the best results you can get in science and math.

Step **2**

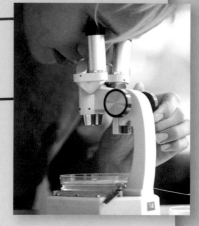

Go to college to get a bachelor of nursing degree. The other option is to apply to a local college to become a Licensed Practical Nurse (LPN), which is usually a year-long employment and training program that mixes theory and clinical experience. After earning a nursing degree, you must also earn your license by passing an exam. You can then work as a nurse and complete further study while on the job. As an LPN, you may receive credit for qualifications and experience if you go on to get an undergraduate degree at a college or university.

Incredible ER

The John H. Stroger Jr. Cook County Hospital is a world-renowned academic medical center in Chicago. It has one of the world's largest and busiest ERs. It treats more than 130,000 adults, 30,000 children, and 4,500 major trauma patients every year.

After completing your nursing degree and becoming a registered nurse, you can apply to study for a specialized graduate diploma in emergency nursing.

Continue studying to keep up with medical, procedural, and technological advances, and gain certificates and credentials in other specialized areas of emergency nursing, such as trauma nursing.

Remember, it takes a certain kind of person to be a nurse, working in sometimes stressful and extreme situations. However, it is also one of the most rewarding careers you can have, making people better and saving lives!

Opportunities for emergency nurses

Nursing can open up a variety of careers and opportunities such as:

- working for charitable organizations in emergencies or disasters
- participating in mass casualty training—doing mock airplane crashes to test emergency procedures
- CBR (chemical, biological, radioactive) training—learning how to handle these specific hazards
- attending conferences around the world
- conducting medical research and presenting your findings

Find Out More

In the Know

- In medieval and early modern medicine, medicinal leeches were used to treat patients. It was thought that the leeches could suck blood out of a patient to balance body fluids when the patient had a fever.

- Skin glue (histoacryline) may be used instead of sutures for some cuts. This means there are no stitches to be removed, and there is less of a chance that infection or scarring will occur. It is also stronger than most stitches.

- Most hospital emergency rooms are open 24 hours a day, seven days a week. Emergency nurses' hours are generally based on a shift roster basis.

- As of May 2007, the U.S. Department of Labor estimates that the average hourly wage for a registered nurse is $30.04, equaling $62,480 a year. The lowest 10 percent earned $42,040, and the highest 10 percent earned more than $87,310.

Further Reading

Brandon, Karen. *Nurse*. Detroit: Blackbirch Press, 2006.

Cunningham, Kevin. *Nurse*. Ann Harbor, Mich.: Cherry Lake Pub., 2009.

Somervill, Barbara A. *Clara Barton: Founder of the American Red Cross*. Minneapolis: Compass Point Books, 2007.

Wick, Elaine. *It's My Future: Should I Be a Nurse Practitioner?* Cherry Hill, N.J.: National Association of Pediatric Nurse Practitioners, 2004.

On the Web

For more information on this topic, use FactHound.
1. Go to *www.facthound.com*
2. Choose your grade level.
3. Begin your search.
This book's ID number is 9780756540784
FactHound will find the best sites for you.

Glossary

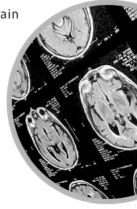

abdomen—front part of the body below the chest; contains the stomach and intestines

anemia—illness caused by having too few red blood cells

anesthesiologists—nurses trained to give anesthetics (painkillers)

cannulas—small, flexible tubes inserted into the body to drain fluids or provide medication

diagnosis—to identify what is wrong with a patient

epidemics—diseases that spread over large areas and affect many people

forceps—long tongs or pincers used by a doctor or nurse

hemorrhaging—serious bleeding, especially inside the body

laceration—torn or ragged wound

oncology—branch of medicine dealing with the treatment of cancer

orthopedic—concerned with disorders and deformities of the skeleton and joints

pediatrics—branch of medicine dealing with the care of children

paramedics—people trained to give emergency treatment, often as part of an ambulance team

radiographers—people trained to operate scans and X-rays

rapid infuser—machine that transports blood into a person's body at a fast rate

resuscitation (resus) bay—area specially equipped for reviving unconscious patients

trauma—physical damage done to the body by an accident or injury

triage—to sort and rank patients on the basis of their needs

ventilator—machine that helps patients breathe

Index

Look for More Books in This Series:

Focusing on Fitness: Have You Got What It Takes to Be a Personal Trainer?

Cordially Invited: Have You Got What It Takes to Be an Event Planner?

Cover Story: Have You Got What It Takes to Be a Magazine Editor?

Cleared for Takeoff: Have You Got What It Takes to Be an Airline Pilot?

Creating Cuisine: Have You Got What It Takes to Be a Chef?

Eyes for Evidence: Have You Got What It Takes to Be a Forensic Scientist?

Going Live in 3, 2, 1: Have You Got What It Takes to Be a TV Producer?

Trendsetter: Have You Got What It Takes to Be a Fashion Designer?

Wild About Wildlife: Have You Got What It Takes to Be a Zookeeper?